Octopus

Octopus
Patrick Warner

BIBLIOASIS
WINDSOR, ON

FIRST EDITION

Library and Archives Canada Cataloguing in Publication

Warner, Patrick, 1963–, author
        Octopus / Patrick Warner.

Poems.

Issued in print and electronic formats.
ISBN 978-1-77196-131-8 (paperback). ISBN 978-1-77196-132-5 (ebook)

        I. Title.

PS8595.A7756O28 2016   C811'.6   C2016-901860-1
                                                                                    C2016-901861-X

Edited by Zachariah Wells
Copy-edited by Allana Amlin
Typeset by Ellie Hastings
Cover designed by Chris Andrechek

Published with the generous assistance of the Canada Council for the Arts and the Ontario Arts Council. Biblioasis also acknowledges the support of the Government of Canada through the Canada Book Fund and the Government of Ontario through the Ontario Book Publishing Tax Credit.

PRINTED AND BOUND IN CANADA

MIX
Paper from
responsible sources
FSC® C004071

CONTENTS

for
Gregory F. Warner
(1921–2015)

OCTOPUS

Just through the door, I gander due west
until arrested by an on-the-go girl, in hairband,
sucking a dumbtit, her freckles all sparkles,

holding before my face her slender hand,
its fingers showing signs of hyperextension
(the slightest pressure would bend

them straight back to her wrist). Her tiny palm
is divided in four by a cross,
each quadrant bearing a postage stamp,

each embossed with a propelling octopus.
"To make you swim where few have swum,"
she says, "a life in ten hours, more or less."

I dab one on the snail-mail of my tongue.
I turn to pay her, but find she has gone,
a wisp inhaled into the club's cavernous lung.

Nothing then, no tingle, nothing until a line
appears—a zigzag of joins through the parquet
floor. I follow, funamble, one step at a time,

between dancers, until my muscles ache,
until suddenly comes a flare of lantern light,
the click of a key in a lock, then the creak

of a barn door letting animals in for the night.
I enter, and there in the doorless first stall
is a plough horse, a grey-dappled white.

His conker eyes have a calming effect.
He holds before my face two lacquered hooves
that he snaps together like halves of a book,

like a prize-fighter tapping black *Everlast* gloves.
All this is a ceremony, preamble
to his presentation—a gesture of love—

of a pearl-white harness. I fall
for it immediately, for its Doris Day fifties' hair,
for it being the corbelled arch a fully

loaded camel would struggle to pass under.
An hour, ten hours or a year has elapsed.
I find myself standing before a mirror:

that octopus *vulgaris*
has injected its lamp-black into my eyeball,
dilating my pupil out into the iris,

like an idea that's inflamed the public will,
breeding a strongman, a movement, an empire,
leaving all but a few wondering what the hell

has transpired. SOS's wired in from everywhere,
again I am with the shuffling masses in the station,
those displaced, who refuse to fight wars,

not from cowardice, but from the lingering notion
that they have never been invested in the place
nor will be. Notion calcifying to conviction,

I pull out my wallet. A one-way ticket, please,
I say to the eight-armed station master
lounging on the other side of the Plexiglas.

FIVE YEARS OLD

Above his cocoa cup, a wisp of steam.
And his coat is there, which can only mean
he is taking a break from blackboard sums,
the rules, the plastic apples, the rustling nuns.

You will find him just around the corner,
in the wing where he is not supposed to go,
staring out across the playground
at concrete two-storeys, all in a row.

He is counting back from five on one hand,
to his council house, fifth from the end,
touching the tip of each finger in turn,
counting backwards from five to confirm.

THE TIGHTROPE WALKER

The grind-organ lady's
Quaker-bearded monkey,
anhedonic elephants,
drugged lions, insouciant
ungulate dromedaries
and belligerent camels
will tomorrow be ushered
into confinement.

With these will go
the washing-machine-cum-
bisected-turbine that spins,
that basin of sticky wisps,
spun stratosphere glomming
on a dipped stick to confect
edible pink insulation.

Stacked like ark runners will be
parenthetical sections
of the two-ring circus,
and with them the big top's
bamboo poles a small boy
named Hal imagined were
fishing rods for whales.

His neck stiff from looking up,
his eyes so long fixed
on the glittering funambulist
he imagines he is up there
with her seeing what she sees
when she looks down:
eyes all gelatin and night,
like frogspawn in a ditch;
workweek complexions, a
shade of pale past exhaustion,
expressions as volatile
as empty naphtha cans.

His stomach floods with butterflies;
butterscotch-coloured they waft
and flutter as Miss Muffet makes
her way on bony
sheep-faced slippered feet
across the braided cable
from tuffet to tuffet.

Later he will be unable to say
when he got carried away
or why he hid in a wicker hamper,
under baguette-sized lace-up
bulb-toed shoes, itchy neon
nylon wigs and red ball noses,
on a bed of oily hawsers,
pegs with hangnail heads,
mauls all dents and nicks.

Tomorrow the pigeon-chested
lion tamer and the tightrope
walker will pick out his cry
from the squawks of macaws,
from the shrieks of parakeets,
from the ratcheting crees of toucans,
and drop him in the next town,
entrusted to the perfumed,
fire-breathing policeman.

STARLING

Cat's jaw shudders like one of his bearings
has busted and clogged his whiskery bushings.
He lets out a strangled gasp and launches
himself against the window glass.

In the bare lilac, a half-robot starling,
his nibs whose song scans shortwave bandwidth,
who keeps a live cicada in his crop,
beneath his iridescent brush-stroked ruff;

one tiny speck from the murmuration
I saw undulate above the lake, until pulled
like iron filings down into a maple tree
that shook with wing beats and roosting chatter.

L'IMMIGRANT

The smell of oranges was all
that would remain of him;
an essence rising from a plate
in a fine hotel, the last strain
of strange before it became
familiar. This was his epitaph.

Departure came with a sense
of peace. Newness negated
the awful fact that he was
dragging a parachute behind
him that would not detach.
For every yank, a yank back.

His attitude would forge
his itinerary, purchase his ticket.
He would not be arrogant:
that way led to atrocity.
He would be brave, luminous.
He would pursue appeasement.

His marriage, when it came,
would be a schism, a sign
that there would be no return,
a thought that reduced
him, made him purge until
he felt he might vanish.

And yet, he had to admit,
that out of this malaise came
promise; such reduction
seemed to pave his way;
seemed to say that all along
this was his plan of attack,

only now he fully grasped it:
to reject was to die, to refuse
was to die, to mock was to die.
The forfeit had to be made
before he could parlay,
he must render from himself

to be restored; he must not
glorify loss but beg pardon
from the life abandoned;
he must refine, not excuse,
live this duplicity not as
saboteur, but as open door.

The Watercourse

The watercourse is a system of meaning
in which the sense of freedom that comes
with being a flowing body depends heavily
on restriction which in worst cases becomes
a prison though mostly it doesn't come
to this because the watercourse has a
release valve by which the cloudiness
of such thought becomes the means of
rescue and by the same process we are
subject to a beneficial downpour with
excess rain collecting as surface runoff
and carrying some surface with it
dipping into drainage basins and joyful
is the thought of groundwater recharge
inspirational the springs the melting
snowpack and glaciers that push the
streams creeks rivulets rills and brooks
as well as burns and becks to natural
confluence with other bodies, salt or sweet.

BLISS

Sunlight flooding through the diesel bus
is the objective correlative for my bliss.
The hard words turn to glass in my mouth.
I let them slide out, like a set of teeth.

It seems some super alloy of irony
that I have emerged on the other side of me
with a burning need to say what I mean
and ignore the voice that undermines:

Such exuberance is proof that I am ill,
in need of a designer pharmaceutical;
the whole episode just a worn-out dream,
the soul to body, as fume to gasoline.

COLD JULY
for Elise Partridge (1958–2015)

1.

I have seen it a beaver-dammed
lukewarm dribble, but this summer the brook's a river,
deep and cold, running steeped tea
and a skim of froth around lichened rocks,
roaring like an air conditioner.

Its white noise is enforced by oversized pines:
their branches albatross
from broom-closet dry to green ends shagged
with cones the colour of peanut skins
and flecked with crystals of sap.

A cindery sentry guards the top:
his ash beak clacking as he hunches
for takeoff, his wings branching
from a light crate core, eyelashing at the tips.
Timber creak in his phlegm-fat caw.

2.

Down on the strand, big surf bangs,
lifting gulls from where they sit
like electric clothes irons. They leave
lead-white splotches,
and webbed wavery wigwams.

A piece of driftwood perfectly catches
the boomerang of a swimmer's arm.
Six-foot kelp bullwhips
have the trapped viscosity of poured motor oil
before they flare to lasagna at the tips.

Out where the ocean betrays
its breathing—closer in than the endless flat,
but farther out than the surf—a whiskery face
rides a swell and watches: time on the Nautilus
would bulk those milk bottle shoulders.

Drawn-tight hoodies small our faces
to beach stone ovals
on which our features perish.
Your message to us was simple:
look closely, and cherish.

DOWNPOUR

A wedge of white foam as though blown
from a sink's cumulus of Palmolive,
signalling the full flume that will soon
overspill to flood the trail bed ankle-deep
with runoff. Strained through bog, it makes
a microbrewery Meister's fantasy: all
ambers and blonds, double stout where
slick black liquorice tree roots steep
in the cut-away bank's mud pool.
Submerged rocks and stones clack
like smacked shot glasses on the slippery
slope of post-work Friday. Everywhere
in the woods it's happy hour. Cistern trickle
becomes a stuck stop-cock's full flush roar
where a normally low-murmur stream
barges in. Clear water bubbles cluster,
seething into froth, building into foam
board insulation. Blown to one side,
fresh fizz coagulates to cappuccino on top
and poked with a stick reveals a crystal
structure underneath, like rotten snow.
Further down, where the grade lessens,
smaller forms persist: oblong doilies;
crocheted antimacassars; gobs of
cuckoo spit; and here where two stones
make a whirlpool, a round lace pastie
ringed by seven clear bubbles—a rotary
phone's finger holes—the whole mass
ticking anticlockwise. New streams

pour glassy through ferns, over mosses,
circumventing stones, laminating grasses,
with all the confidence of adolescence.
Here, a fast-moving rivulet breaches
a hex of twigs to leave a snake track
or a trials-bike tyre tattoo on the surface
of the trail-bed stream. And here, in the
small gorge, the smooth monk's pate
of the half-submerged spherical stone
I often stop to look down upon
(marvel at its Zen garden perfection)
is eclipsed by the torrent, but tomorrow
will have risen again from its clear
pool, its circumference smaller by
an angstrom or nanometer, its position
liberally skewed toward fresh views.

Umbrellas

Remember when I took blank Scrabble tiles
and pushed them into the earth in that pot
of fungi you kept on the bedside table,
depressing them until they were one-third

buried and resembled marble headstones
next to the umbrellas of the bereaved?
In those days I could turn bleakly inward
at a moment's notice. But you would have

none of it. Hush, you'd say, pointing out
the scope of the umbrella, how beneath
its canopy there is always space for two.
Where are you, Mary Poppins, when I need you?

ANNE SEXTON

Her need is fevered. She arranges time and place,
makes a date with an imaginary lover.
She pulls the blind's tough nylon string;
the cord and pulley make a zipper sound.
The beige slats climb, fusing into one.

She thinks of the tree house in her garden,
the insect songs of summer in childhood,
pulling the rope ladder up behind her.
She will sit for a while and watch the weather,
Wait for a break in the clouds, an aperture.

Even now the thought of being alone
sends a tingle clean through to the bone,
that delicious feeling of apprehension,
the patient presence there of someone.
It was never a question of where but whom.

Sunlight colanders in diagonal beams
through sixteen-pane high windows. One skein,
swirling with chalk dust, cleat dust and skin,
catches her full in the face. Closing her eyes
she is absolved. Back in the warm room

she basks in peachiness, still as a stone.
All words are profane in this pedagogical
silence (which is the antithesis of violence).
But nothing good can stay. A door opens,
and time, the headmaster, calls her back in.

A war veteran, his stump arm points to four,
while his good arm raised above his head
holds a bamboo cane. He splits her name
and with oily sibilance fits its parts between
the major and minor clause in archaic syntax

he primes with years of formal education
before loading all into the canon of his diction,
scattering it to the four winds. Oh Father,
she says, and darts her eyes to the left,
at something running away from her,

her courage, obscenely naked, which she
can only find again through pantomime,
through poetry, though every poem she writes
sounds the same, dulled by savagery
of thinking, and beaten down by blame,

over and over the same cold prophesy.
This tree is your hand one day in the future.
These leaves are all that is left of your clothes
after the brain shocks and chemical torture.
These are the first boozy veins on your nose.

Over and over the same smeared vision:
The streets are empty, still and wet.
The afternoon fog has an inner glow
as though about to reveal a secret:
something she knows or once had known.

The streets are empty, still, sacramental;
the decision, long fraught, is finally taken.
Open your mouth and swallow that handful;
sleep in the truth until you awaken.

MARTINI

I'm too young to have heard of Dorothy Parker.
If you ask me what a martini is, I will say it's
Tom Thumb's smaller cousin, Martin.
If you ask me what is under
my
host,
I will
say
my
Catholic tongue.

THE OLD

The water stain climbs slowly up his shorts
to wet his belly. Ferns of white chest hair float out
before him. His beard dips, now his chin,
lips, cheeks; his eyes close. He's gone.

I dedicate this poem to the old everywhere,
to kin who no longer know one another,
to systems which save us from the bother
of soiling our hands with adult diapers.

I feel sick, then glee. I feel a wave of empathy
freeing a sublimated desire to break free
of all that once crushed me:
Let's eliminate the old entirely.

Meat Puppet

The form shows slots where wings could attach:
these are not slots for wings but the spots where fins
were hacked off. Now flipper-less, the shark sinks,
knitting billowing sleeves of red-pink, its pen-light eye
winking white, as it slips into fathomless depths.

In the barn, big knuckles choke a spring chicken,
or slim porcelain hands slip a cock's neck
between cleaver and block. Later in May,
fat woolly lambs will be shushed into pens,
their big bleats bled with a pass of the knife.

And it's all for a shank, for a hock, fresh liver or chops,
for a T-bone, a sirloin, a rump steak, a roast,
for a tongue cut out at the root and displayed,
curled back on itself like a spring, set on a rack
on a tray, its stippled taste buds like tiny florets.

Sometimes at night I wake with a start, I rattle
in dark, all covered in sweat, feel the terrible fear
of beasts as they run the slaughterhouse gauntlet,
I can't help but recall old jittery newsreels,
babushkas with bundles herded at gunpoint.

It's supposed to be black and white, but it's not—
when I think what happens to cats in the houses of drunks,
in rooms full of boys filled with bloodlust and fear—
it's not black and white, not at all, it's vivid,
3D and full colour. It fills me with horror.

And all for a city squirming with people, a province
too big for its britches, a country flexing its borders,
for the step, the lectern, the pulpit, the stage,
the mics arranged in bouquets, the crackling PA,
the strongman fisting his dummy: the people.

My mouth swamps with spit and my stomach turns
over. I fall on my knees; profess my love
for the animal kingdom, promise never to eat them,
nor harm them, promise once and for all to break
ranks with my brothers in fur, my sisters in feather,

to find peace in my hide with the herd.
But weeks go by and I sink into sad lethargy—
sure I feel lighter and faster, sure my eyes shine,
my digestion's never been swifter or cleaner,
but something of heft and substance is missing.

I know what is it but I'd rather not say,
and it builds and it builds and soon comes the day
I tuck into a chicken breast saddled with bacon,
or a tome-thick striploin blackened with pepper.
And with every morsel I become more human,

with each mastication I am more a nation,
with each chewed bolus I swallow my pleasure.
And whatever guilt or shame I might feel
is complex and simple as textures and flavours:
as the thought that I could rise above nature.

Heartfelt Psalm

I kill myself a little bit to live,
to stop the flywheel, the numbers flicking,
to reset the clock to zero Eden,
create the right conditions for return.

I woke today so full of feeling—
so full of love for everyone I'd failed,
so overflowing with good intentions—
I woke up certain that I had a soul.

Free from pressures that had pressed me thin,
I slipped into a new dimension,
out of reach of the selfish one within,
walking softly there for fear I'd wake him.

THE PHILOSOPHY OF NO

No pushed the pebble that had been forming
at the top of my larynx for some time,
rolled it up over the back of my tongue.
I tasted sourness—like the pith in a plumb—

which only increased each time I brought it up.
I had tried swallowing it, to no avail—
perhaps I was afraid that stomach acid
would prove its topsoil, that it would root in bile.

Soon a mass would cuckoo my gut,
block my esophagus. My joints would stiffen,
start to burn and then refuse to bend.
In late winter I would meet my end.

There was nothing for it but to give it air.
Still, knowing its volcanic reputation,
its legendary ability to end a conversation,
I made the smallest, softest mouth I could

as I expressed it. The world faded to a blank.
What sustained me was the story of a drunk
who woke one day facing a white wall
and thought he'd been struck blind.

The world was one unpeopled wasteland,
a whiteout driven by the howling wind.
Perhaps I am overstating the case a bit.
Slowly, shapes began to take form.

Soon there appeared a desk and a chair,
a brass cage polished to shiniest gold.
Everything looked new or refurbished.
For sale stickers were stuck with sold.

The door was ajar. Through it I could see
a velvet rope line and a queue of people.
All looked scrubbed, in their Sunday bests,
mindful of manners, as for an interview.

I was happy to see them, saw no problem
admitting the rug as well as the side table,
the nuclear family, even distant kin.
In this way the empty world filled in.

Choke

Trapping it between middle and index fingers,
he pulled back the plunger. "This modifies
the air pressure in the intake manifold,
altering the ratio of fuel and air quantity,

and prevents the engine from stopping dead."
He could see from the way I looked at him
I was in over my head. "Like punctuation," he said,
"introduced into a line where meaning

is overwhelmed by too much emotion,
some jumped-up-pumped-up rhythmic flow
that has at its core a dubious notion:
The heart of hearts knows all there is to know."

Resuscitation

The paddles make his chest rise and fall.
His stopped heart kicks, starts to beat again.
They bring him back to life because they can,
because no one thought to sign a DNR.

His beating heart beats evenly again,
and the crash-cart team marvel at his age.
Because no one thought to sign a DNR,
the doctors will not let him turn the page.

They marvel at my ancient father's age—
what's resuscitation if not resurrection?
They will not let my father turn the page.
They hide inside a world of protocol.

This resuscitation is no resurrection.
They bring him back to life because they can.
They hide inside a world of protocol.
The paddles make his chest rise and fall.

FATBERG

"It's a clot, a clog, an obstruction,
a jam up, a blockage, a dam," he said,
piling on the synonyms to emphasize
his point that anxiety can blow
one's thinking out of proportion.

"It's no bus-sized fatberg either,"
he continued, opening the tall cabinet,
"but the result of all the little spills,
hastily wiped up over the years.
The cure is really quite mechanical."

He shook before my face a plunger,
a drain auger, the air burst canister.
Sot to my nervous system, this last
was enough to activate the pores
around my hairline and in the alcoves

behind my ears, setting in motion
little trolley cars of sweat,
their fast cool trickles, slow turns.
"Mostly it boils down (forgive
the puns) to this insoluble fact:

wet wipes cling to fat, and fat
coagulates ego. There may be
some sanitary products as well,
condoms, hair of course, fruit even,
and there are always goldfish.

I'd recommend some herbal tea,
one hot cup to be drunk on the hour.
And as you sip that aromatic brew
you may feel a shift in your POV,
sudden release from a mild case

of locked-in syndrome. Euphoria
will follow as you take on the news
that you have suffered for years
from a self-inflicted curse which
thinking about has made worse:

you are not the centre of the universe."

MATERIALIST

I pick up the figurative barbecue lighter
and push it all the way down his throat
until I locate what I am looking for:
the man who sits alone and without hope

within the ribbed grotto of his sternum,
cross-legged and pot-bellied, an icon,
though not at all like the enlightened one,
but dulled with negative expectation.

I flick the switch, turn him into a torch.
But he doesn't believe in a figurative sun;
he simply lays aside his sandwich,
thumps his chest to signal heartburn.

THE PHILOSOPHY OF YES

If no was a stone, it was a stone flung.
Yes was the jacket of breeze it put on.
Yes had a velvet velocity
and the fist in that force was a fuse.

A thumbnail striking a sulphurous mood
made a spark, set the line fizzling
and spitting, consuming not only itself
but the notion of boundary

as it sizzled to barrels, filled to the brim
with sodium chlorate and sugar,
wedged in the wall of the icy ruckus
that all spring long had blocked the pass.

The spot vacated by yes was a purr,
sweet as a chauffeured antique car,
as the back-seat pamphlet promising a tour,
as far as I wanted, in any direction.

Yes breezed around, oh so casual,
said don't fuss, don't fret the detail,
example: not lavender, but a sea of purple.
There are no names, only people.

It said look far out but not far in.
Ignore that curtain dropped suddenly,
the figure—shaped like a swastika—
glimpsed hiding in a tree.

I'm not sure when I began to notice
that every turn we made was a right one,
which meant we were travelling in circles,
if circles can be made from angles.

This became a point of contemplation
until I mentioned it to the driver
who pulled a U-turn in one greased motion.
All his turns after that were left ones.

At the sharpest bends I saw small groups
of men in uniform—border guards,
I assumed, though hard to be certain,
thrown as I was in the opposite direction.

BUBBLE

His mood that day was black, overwrought,
as subtle and supple as a football boot,
something worn in more than worn out.
His temper was such he would never give up.

And what it hatched was a shining bubble,
the kind that children blow from rings,
or pull in streams from wands as they run
screaming, a simple soap and water film.

A globe shimmering under the weight
of its being, it filled him with superstition:
He dared not reach for this fragile thing,
this nothing shaped as could have been.

GUERRILLA

Adios to my pueblo, my adobe abode,
my white-washed hacienda of the mind.
Adios to the crucible of my culture,
its carbonado bellowsed red hot
(like my *cajones* when I remember you,
my *mestizo mujer*, my gordita).

Adios to the good luck of my birth,
my vain companions, conquistador class.
Adios to the bad luck that shifted
my ballast (the bones of the Taino)
and sent to the bottom my galleon,
those bubbles roiling like laughter.

Adios to incommunicado, that place
where every amigo turned stranger
and every stranger became both
vigilante and judge exiling me,
with an alligator smile, to another
term in the diaspora, my Alcatraz.

Adios to my bodega, my damp cellar
in the barrio of small fry, to my dream
of being caballero or gaucho,
breaker of mustangs, and not just
a buckaroo on a burro, corral clown,
lassoing slack-jawed alpacas.

Adios to the dengue of that decade,
to pinpointing time and place,
the precise features of my peccadillo.
Those thoughts like mosquitos, pimento.
Adios to being (in hindsight) Quixotic.
Adios to playing apache to myself.

Hello instead to my barren cedilla,
(this elsewhere) which is no nada,
this solitude which can be a fiesta.
Hello to the riches that are at hand,
the bounty of the land visible to eyes
not fixed on some distant star.

Hello to anchovies and fried bananas,
to barbecued blackened barracuda,
roasted iguana seasoned with chipotle,
cilantro or jalapeño, or my favourite,
paella-fried peccary with potato.
And afterwards, in the cool night,

ambling like an armadillo, following
coyote tracks along the camino
to the bottom of the canyon,
(far below the green chaparral,
below the mesa and the savanna)
to the arroyo where I fill my pail.

The Prize

The prize this year goes not to the victim,
not to the faithful who stuck to one tune,
not to the critic, who should have known better,
who was placed in a pot of cold mutton stew

and awoke to find it had started to bubble;
this year the medal, all golden and shiny,
goes to the one who witnessed the priest
molesting the boy in full view of his family,

a sight that froze them hard in their places.
Oh, the incredulous looks on their faces.
The new Father, they said, is a good bit of fun.
The prize this year is awarded to no one.

FOG

The romantic trades in his black beret
for a shower cap poofed like a chef's hat.

The shale path up the side of the hill
feels like a sideburn unshaven.

All my thoughts turn inward
like thoughts before a mirror.

Palette-shaped shapes in the sink
show up the water's laminate edge.

The stopper's an unopened water-lily
flower. Pulled, it pulls a long rope:

In the amphibian's kitchen a bell
ringing sends a ripple, a pulse

through khaki, black-spotted skins,
palpitating egg-cream food-baby bellies;

the amber-eyed frogs glance up
from their knitting—frond fingers stilled

on clear pearls for the Emperor's cloak.
Have you tried this new moisturizer?

How should I tell the story of no place
and the life I spent there with no one?

The bathroom is a low-ceilinged bubble,
six feet wide. Everything within its

shallow-field focus glares,
HD revealing more than is there:

Tangerine bath balls are as airplane
aisle-path lights; the blueberry

beads' high-cirrus surfaces suggest
they are canisters of dry ice;

the shower curtains' conifer decals
(on clear days a blur), find sharp silhouettes;

their shag tops are thickets of foreign
antennas on a flotilla of off-white RVs

and media trucks permitted to park
at the site of this wonder/disaster.

Here, where sweat meets the cool,
at the perimeter where corners dissolve,

I share with the fog a last cigarette
(king-size, menthol), and listen

to the rale the obscured ocean makes,
steadily dragging its body ashore.

BLACK

The stone was not a mirror; it was a screen,
which made what I saw a projection.
This surface had committed no error
in capturing everything in the room but me.

So nothing was wrong. I was not there.
There was no substance to my being.
Because I had no self, I saw no one,
and having no depth, I perceived none.

Behind that screen no one had gathered,
no ancestors, no future generation.
In that obsidian, black as terror,
there was only the echo of superstition.

SOME CORN

A narrow swath in the corn field sways.
Some low animal is slinking its way,
brushing stalks with its flanks. The ears
are muffled under husks and silk-string cloth.

The pin-head cobs knock heads together,
trade thoughts, as though they were watched,
as though they are afraid to say. They find
camouflage in corny gags and cliché.

Self-consciousness is not quite performance,
which is to be some other, and afterwards
go through withdrawal, feel the green leaves
pulled back, the stacked bullion exposed,

the yellow strings lying about uselessly
as though a parachute had been cut away.
Was it by chance that you came to be here?
This is the theory propounded by corn.

But the sky is so blue this June morning
and the bicolour su so high and so green.
And who is it wanders now through the ranks?
Some debutante, eyes out on stalks,

whacked still from the Mason jar of water
left unattended at the party. Her every thought
a non sequitur, making her feel at one
with the wonder-jammed oneness of the world.

Golden Acres

The clippers, the ones with maple handles,
should be wiped with oil when you're finished
and returned to their place in the shed,
between the T-square and the spirit level.

Stand the lump hammer beside the axe,
under the row of masonry chisels,
by the box with the whetstone and hand awl.
The rods for the chimney brushes are stacked

in the corner: bamboo poles with brass connectors.
You'll need them when the drain stops: use the pinch bar
to pry up the third flagstone from the shore,
the claw works best for clogs of paper.

*

I remember shooting a few jackdaws alright.
The buggers used to build nests in the flue,
drop sticks down. What was I supposed to do?
Sit tight until they set the chimney alight?

I don't remember that I ever shot a cat
through the gate in, as you say, "the wee small hours."
Those pocks you say you saw along the bars
were likely rust blisters that popped their caps.

The cat you're thinking of—the one I killed—
was the tabby that crawled inside the sewer
after being hit on the road by a tractor.
I cocked the gun and gave him both barrels.

*

When it's your turn to clean up the kitchen
make sure you wipe the counter down as well.
Use the leather rag to mop both windows and sills.
It's always a battle there with condensation.

After you have a shower remember to tighten
the plastic bag back around the shower head
by pulling the drawstring. You'd be amazed
how fast drips will turn the sides of the bath green.

Before going to bed, cover up the television
with the old table cloth, the paisley pattern.
Check to see if Pinky is out or if he's in.
If he's in, put the litter box down for him.

*

The night nurse here is a bitch on wheels.
Before going to bed, cover up the television
with the old table cloth, the paisley pattern.
Take care of things and they will serve you well.

You might call this an existential question—
I think that I've been stupid all my life,
made gullible by the church, by belief—
but how could all the dead fit into heaven?

D'you see that old one slumped in the chair?
She keeps asking if this is the mental.
When I was a young buck I used to cycle
miles on a Sunday to court her older sister.

*

Cars were scarce back then—not yet a habit.
You went by bike or by foot or not at all.
I'd cycle from Portumna out to Ballyshrule
on a summer evening to hunt for rabbits.

Oh the freedom of dogs running alongside us—
my terrier—Scutty Boy—he was a terror—
tearing through the demesne, by the derelict manor,
over the swing bridge and out to Terryglass,

or over through Lurra to Borrisokane—
there's a rhyme we used to have as children:
"Nothing for nothing from Borrisokane,
Come to Portumna and you'll get the same."

                    *

There's a musical little keypad on the door,
the one just to the right of the nurse's station.
To go out you have to know the combination.
Play it by ear said the nurse when I asked her.

They say this place is built in the field—
the one right in front of the big stone house—
that used to be the protestant minister's place.
At my time of life beliefs are lightly held.

But they're a decent crowd here all the same.
There's always seconds, dessert after dinner.
Afterwards, I sit and read the paper.
They tell me I read the same one all the time.

                    *

They serve tea on the hour. It's always Earl
Grey. What's that—a leopard? No, it's a cheetah,
going hell for leather after some poor creature.
The cheetah's eyes are round, pretty like a girl's.

Slung between shoulders and hips, its body
would remind you a bit of a four-poster bed,
but with the springs shot—aye, swaybacked.
Look at it now with its chops all bloody,

and the springbok or is it a Thompson's Gazelle?
Ah, Jaysus Christ, it's been eaten alive.
That's nature for you. That's nature alright.
Give me the yoke and I'll change the channel.

TASTE
for Greta

In size somewhere between the tide pool's
stacked rank of blue-black blanks
for Zuki's nail shop, and biceps bivalves
bunched on hydrothermal vents.

Most of them tight-lipped, maybe a dozen
razor-clammed open or octopus tripped
to show the nacreous inner sanctum,
the hallowed aftermath of confession.

The fork-shucked occupant a tiny snot gut
of smoky orange sin you rolled over your
tongue, not sure whether you should
upchuck or find a way to be enlightened.

PATH

Alder-flanked
at first,
then shin-
high shrubs,
dog
rose and Labrador
tea
I beat the dew
from
with a
bleached, bone-dry
flotsam stick, my
aspergillum
polka-
dotting
the root-
gauzed earth
that percussive
footfalls
sound
out as peat.

Near the top,
a forgotten
grey
hoodie
slung
on a boulder
blends in so
well I think
this devil-ma-
care

erratic
has shrugged
off
the yoke
of function
and
grown a style.

The bald rock
summit,
scored
with glacier sled
runners,
shelters
clumps of moss,
crisp on top,
that squelch
beneath
like abandoned bowls
of breakfast cereal.

Later, the low
sun sends
a single beam
through
aisles
of trees,
cutting
the dusk
like an usher's
torch.

HOUSE

Travelling to return I find the house more fit,
more itself, with little flourishes
I'd never noticed, with unfinished
edges I accept like tics,

places where love catches; the wood frame
creaking in south winds, the timbers
reminiscing trees, a sense that in among
the seasoned joists there's green

wood still, primed to bud. How comical
it seems now, a thought to make you laugh
on the verge of sleep, drawing
you back, before you settle down again.

ABANDONMENT

In retrospect, we were right to hesitate
before bending over to pick one up,
because that first mouthful set us on a path
from which there was no turning back.

The free booty both sated and whetted:
more raspberries sliced in thin batons,
flecked with cock's eggs and cocoa nibs;
more salty interiors, enrobed in milk chocolate.

Our swollen nascent senses awakened
to pears and grapes that everywhere hung,
distended from tree and vine; to rabbits
that could be dispatched with a stick;

to ranks of pink-spotted trout stacked
in the wavering pool, in such numbers
that a rock carelessly flung would send
a stunned handful belly up to the bank.

We learned togetherness was hunger
that fed on little pat-a-cakes of wonder
that popped up overnight, on either
side of the grassy path, like mushrooms.

In what felt like a day, we advanced
farther and further, passing through bramble
and briar into the heart of the forest,
coming at last to a clearing

where stood a dome-shaped house
made entirely from bones.
Arms entwined, hands clutching,
we went forward to look, peered over

the femur sill, past the flung open
shutters of ribs, to find this heat-struck
cottage garden in mid-summer,
a blackbird singing, bees hovering

over high stems, beneath which
we saw our own huddled forms,
woven through with trumpet vine,
silver hair still clinging to our skulls.

Acknowledgements

Thanks and love to Rochelle. Thanks to everyone at Biblioasis, especially to Zach Wells. Thanks also to the editors of the following magazines: *The Manchester Review, Riddle Fence, Prism International, Southward Journal, The Malahat Review, The Walrus, Arc Magazine, The Stinging Fly,* and *The Fiddlehead.*

PATRICK WARNER has published four collections of poetry: *All Manner of Misunderstanding*; *There, There*; *Mole*; and *Precious*. He has twice won the E.J. Pratt Poetry Prize. Warner grew up in Claremorris, County Mayo, Ireland. He immigrated to Canada in 1980 and since then has mostly lived in St. John's, Newfoundland.